BEING AN ACTIVE CITIZEN
SERVING ON A JURY

by Vincent Alexander

JURY SELECTION COMMISSION
CRIMINAL JUSTICE CENTER

JURY DUTY SUMMONS

DO NOT DISCARD

pogo

Ideas for Parents and Teachers

Pogo Books let children practice reading informational text while introducing them to nonfiction features such as headings, labels, sidebars, maps, and diagrams, as well as a table of contents, glossary, and index.

Carefully leveled text with a strong photo match offers early fluent readers the support they need to succeed.

Before Reading

- "Walk" through the book and point out the various nonfiction features. Ask the student what purpose each feature serves.
- Look at the glossary together. Read and discuss the words.

Read the Book

- Have the child read the book independently.
- Invite him or her to list questions that arise from reading.

After Reading

- Discuss the child's questions. Talk about how he or she might find answers to those questions.
- Prompt the child to think more. Ask: Do you know anyone who has served on a jury? What was the experience like?

Pogo Books are published by Jump!
5357 Penn Avenue South
Minneapolis, MN 55419
www.jumplibrary.com

Copyright © 2019 Jump!
International copyright reserved in all countries. No part of this book may be reproduced in any form without written permission from the publisher.

Library of Congress Cataloging-in-Publication Data

Names: Alexander, Vincent, author.
Title: Serving on a jury : being an active citizen / by Vincent Alexander.
Description: Minneapolis : Jump!, Inc., 2018. Includes bibliographical references and index.
Identifiers: LCCN 2018007467 (print)
LCCN 2018008619 (ebook)
ISBN 9781641280211 (ebook)
ISBN 9781641280198 (hardcover : alk. paper)
ISBN 9781641280204 (pbk.)
Subjects: LCSH: Jury duty–United States–Juvenile literature. Jury–United States–Juvenile literature.
Classification: LCC KF8972 (ebook)
LCC KF8972 .A74 2018 (print)
DDC 347.73/752–dc23
LC record available at https://lccn.loc.gov/2018007467

Editor: Kristine Spanier
Book Designer: Anna Peterson

Photo Credits: moodboard/Getty, cover, 5; Mike Flippo/Shutterstock, 1; Creativeye99/iStock, 3; Sheri Armstrong/Shutterstock, 4; Phanie/Phanie/Superstock, 6-7; RichLegg/Getty, 8-9; LiliGraphie/Shutterstock, 10(frame); GraphicaArtis/Getty, 10(painting); Chris Ryan/Getty, 11; IPGGutenbergUKLtd/iStock, 12-13; Image Source/iStock, 14-15; Spencer Grant/Superstock, 16; Monkey Business Images/Shutterstock, 17; Guy Cali/Getty, 18-19; dcdebs/iStock, 20-21; Africa Studio/Shutterstock, 23.

Printed in the United States of America at Corporate Graphics in North Mankato, Minnesota.

TABLE OF CONTENTS

CHAPTER 1

A FAIR JURY

What happens when someone is charged with a crime? Or has a **dispute** with another person that can't be resolved? They may go to **trial**. A fair trial is a basic right in the United States.

courthouse

Trials happen in the **court** system. Is a charge or claim true? A **jury** decides.

jury

summons ·····▶

JURY DUTY SUMMONS

DO NOT DISCARD

JURY SELECTION COMMISSION
CRIMINAL JUSTICE CENTER

How are jurors chosen?
Usually from a list of voters.
A **summons** is sent.
The person who receives
it must report for duty.

DID YOU KNOW?

Can anyone serve on a jury? No.
Jurors must be at least 18 years old.
They must be **legal citizens**.

18+

Many people are summoned.
Not all are selected. Why?
Attorneys want to find
people who are fair.

They ask questions.
Like what? Do you know
anyone in the trial?
Have you read a lot
about the case? Do you
already have an opinion
about it? Many are excused.

attorney

CHAPTER 2

CRIMINAL AND CIVIL TRIALS

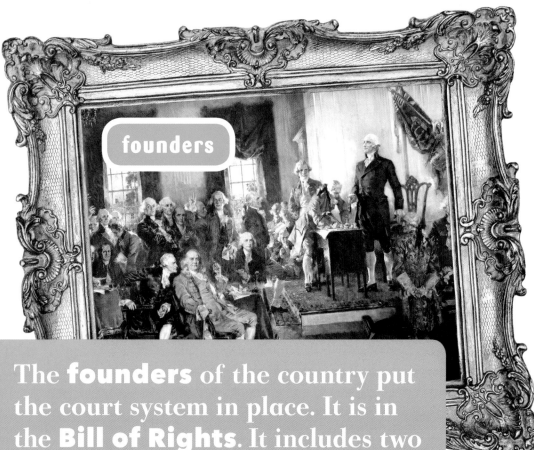

founders

The **founders** of the country put the court system in place. It is in the **Bill of Rights**. It includes two kinds of trials. Criminal and civil.

What is a criminal trial? It involves someone charged with a crime. Civil trials are about disputes.

The jury for a criminal trial usually has 12 people. Alternates are chosen, too. Civil trials usually have only six people. A balanced jury is important. What should be balanced? Gender. Race. Age. Income.

WHAT DO YOU THINK?

Juries are made up of men and women. Rich and poor. Young and old. This is a "jury of one's peers." Why do you think this is important?

The jury must pay close attention. They watch. They listen.

Attorneys present **evidence**. It could be photos. Objects. Documents. Police reports. It might be statements from others. They are known as witnesses.

evidence

CHAPTER 3

THE VERDICT

Now it's time to reach a decision. The jury needs to know about laws, too. The judge explains the laws to them.

judge ·····▶

Next, they choose a foreperson. Then the jury discusses the trial. Does everyone have a chance to talk? The foreperson makes sure.

foreperson

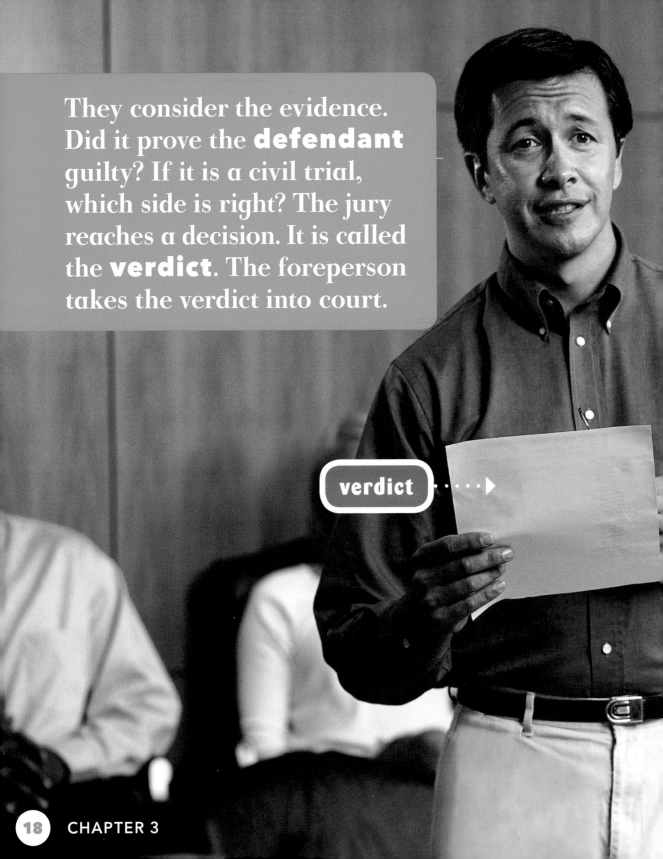

They consider the evidence. Did it prove the **defendant** guilty? If it is a civil trial, which side is right? The jury reaches a decision. It is called the **verdict**. The foreperson takes the verdict into court.

verdict ·····▶

TAKE A LOOK!

· ·

Jury trials usually follow the same steps.

> **A jury is chosen.**

> **Attorneys give opening statements.**
> **Witnesses provide testimonies. Attorneys give closing arguments.**
> **The jury receives instructions from the judge.**

IN A CRIMINAL TRIAL:	**IN A CIVIL TRIAL:**

The jury deliberates. It reaches a verdict. Has the defendant been found guilty?	**The jury deliberates. It decides the outcome of the trial. Should money or property be awarded?**

YES	**NO**	**YES**	**NO**
The jury is excused. The judge determines the **sentence.**	The jury is excused. The defendant is free.	The jury determines the amount. The jury is excused.	The jury is excused.

The jury's verdict is final. The judge can't change it. But the verdict can be **appealed**. A higher court may hear the case later.

Juries keep the legal system working. How? People work together to reach decisions. Serving is a way to be an active citizen.

WHAT DO YOU THINK?

In a criminal trial, the whole jury must agree on the verdict. Civil trials are different. In some states, only a certain number must agree. Why do you think everyone must agree in a criminal trial?

ACTIVITIES & TOOLS

SELECTING A FAIR JURY

Attorneys look for a fair jury. They interview potential jurors. Why? To find jurors who are unbiased, honest, and fair. Find a trial in the news. If it is a criminal trial, what is the defendant charged with? If it is a civil trial, what is the dispute about? Pay attention to the details of the trial.

Then prepare questions. If you were the prosecuting attorney in a criminal trial, what would you ask? If you were defending the person who has been charged with the crime, how would your questions be different? If you were representing someone in a civil trial, what would you ask?

Write your questions in a notebook. Continue to follow the trial in the news. What verdict does the jury reach? Based on the evidence, why do you think the jurors made that decision? Do you agree with it? Why or why not?

GLOSSARY

appealed: Brought to a higher court for a change in a legal decision.

attorneys: People who have studied the law and are trained to advise people and represent them in court.

Bill of Rights: The first ten amendments to the U.S. Constitution, which define the rights that protect every American.

court: A place where legal cases are heard and decided.

defendant: A person who is accused of a crime in a criminal case or is sued in a civil case.

dispute: A disagreement about an issue.

evidence: Information and facts that help prove something is true or false.

founders: People who created the structure and first laws of the United States.

jury: A group of people who listen to the facts at a trial and decide whether the accused person is guilty or innocent.

legal citizens: People who are born in the United States or have been given the rights of U.S. citizenship.

sentence: A punishment given to someone who has been found guilty in court.

summons: An order to appear in a court of law.

testimonies: Spoken statements that are given by people under oath and are submitted as evidence.

trial: The examination of evidence in a court of law to decide if a charge or claim is true.

verdict: The decision of a jury on whether the accused person is guilty or innocent.

INDEX

TO LEARN MORE

Learning more is as easy as 1, 2, 3.

1) Go to www.factsurfer.com
2) Enter "servingonajury" into the search box.
3) Click the "Surf" button to see a list of websites.

With factsurfer, finding more information is just a click away.